To: Phillip,

THE COLOURFUL BLACK AUCTIONEER

Biography of Andrew W Thomas (1856-1924)

I hope you enjoy reading this.

Regards,

Bode Thomas Jr.

Andrew Wilkinson Thomas
1856–1924

THE COLOURFUL BLACK AUCTIONEER
Biography of Andrew W Thomas (1856-1924)

Kunle Thomas

London

Published by Top Agenda Publishing
October 2007

Copyright © 2007, Kunle Thomas

The right of Kunle Thomas to be identified as the author of this work has been asserted by him in accordance with the Copyright, Designs and Patents Act 1988.

ISBN: 978-0-9556505-0-5

All rights reserved. No part of this publication may be reproduced in any material form (including photocopying or storing in any medium by electronic means and whether or not transiently or incidentally to some other use of this publication) without the written permission of the copyright holder except in accordance with the provision of the Copyright, Designs and Patents Act 1988 or under the terms of a licence issued by the Copyright Licensing Agency Ltd, 90 Tottenham Court Road, London W1T 4LP, UK, without the permission in writing of the publisher. Requests to the publisher should be addressed in writing to: Top Agenda Publishing, 7th Floor, Hannibal House, Elephant & Castle, London SE1 6TE, UK or by e-mail to info@topagenda.co.uk

The information contained in this book has been thoroughly researched, to the best of the author's ability. However, the author and publisher cannot provide legal or absolute guarantees and do not accept responsibility for any loss, material or otherwise, arising from the use of information contained in this book.

This book is dedicated to the loving memory of my father
Tinuola Babatunde Thomas
29 April 1917 – 18 May 2007

Ode to 'Anduru'

Back, way back
Eight decades and four, you left
Your country remembers you
Can the world now be celebrating you?

Your sea shore footprints remain
Large and bold they show
They defy sea waves, whirl wind
Was that you they named the hurricane after?

When our race's light was dim, you sparkled
When our knees were bent, you stood tall
Your little hammer, ever busy, ever hot
But how come it never melted?

You led our church
You fought our rights
Mansion, money, honey
Were you really that perfect?

Ah, those footprints
They glow, they guide
They inspire, they …
How can your big shoes ever fit?

© Kunle Thomas

October 2007

Contents

Foreword	9
Preface	11
Acknowledgements	12
About the author	13
Family background and the Oyo royalty	15
Last with lasting legacy – meet Chief Bode Thomas and siblings	25
Trust me; you don't want to see Andy	39
The auctioneer is born	45
Petesi Anduru	57
Better build Bethel big: championing 'Africanism' in the church	61
Safeguarding civil rights: membership of Aborigine's Protection Society	67
Not lost, but gone before' – will, wealth, death	71
Notes	78
Bibliography	81

FOREWORD

I was privileged to read the manuscript before it was published, and it took me on a journey. A journey, not just through time but also through hard work, tribulations, success, religious faithfulness, misdemeanours, celebration, happiness, sadness and mourning. I reflected over different phases of Andrew W Thomas' life vis-à-vis the socio-political climate of his native Nigeria. Born into royalty, yet he had to work hard, from one administrative position to another. Even the native chiefs were not shielded from the harsh realities of colonial rule – after centuries of slavery. It felt as if he was born with a silver plated spoon in his mouth, but was determined - like an alchemist - to turn it into real gold, and I think he did just that. I suspect his royalty must have secured him one or two favours, but he was – by and large, a self-made man.

Kunle has rescued an important piece of history, not just for Nigerians but for black communities globally. For Andrew Thomas to be awarded the contract of auctioning the vast assets of Germany as part of the British and Allied Forces' First World War efforts was a rare achievement for a black man anywhere in the world at that time. I was equally fascinated by his civil rights work. Though the book did not provide much details of his specific role in this area, the fact that he was Vice President of the Aborigines Protection Society, Lagos affiliate, adds to his impressive 'CV'.

His presidency of the African Church Bethel, Lagos, and the deeper implication of the 'break away' from the Church Missionary Society (CMS) at the time of colonial rule was, as Kunle once put it, "a mustard seed for self rule".

Not many black people could travel from Africa or the Caribbean to

Europe towards the end of the 19th century or the early part of the 20th to attend trade exhibitions or for business. Andrew Thomas did just that. Yet to remember that he was just a clerk like many others years earlier, but propelled himself into a profession he knew would bring out the best in him. That was an inspirational move that is worth emulating. He took a leap of faith and achieved his own personal success against the odds.

Now, that man they called Captain Ross. The local administrator (or whatever his title was) who was slapping natives and even some junior chiefs at will. How dare him! Sadly, even today, we still have occasions where similar things happen. However, due to the ongoing efforts of dedicated people, progress has been made in racial relations since the era of Captain Ross.

I enjoyed reading the book, and learnt a bit of Yoruba in the process. Kunle's style of writing makes historical facts as interesting and easy to read as fiction. Some bits made me laugh, some bits inspire and some other parts shocking and sad. Yet, every bit of it is fact and adds to my knowledge of black history.

I wish every reader an enjoyable experience.

Lorna Stewart
Chair, Black History Month 2007
University of the Arts London

PREFACE

Let me start with a little true story. In 1981, I attended a students' bursary interview while getting ready to proceed to the final year of my 'A level' programme at King's College, Lagos. One of the main criteria was that applicants must be an indigene of the awarding state. The interview panel was made up of three people, the oldest I guess was in his 70's. The first question I was asked after telling them my name was: 'which Thomas is yours?' My response was 'Andrew Thomas'. Immediately, the oldest man on the panel jumped up and asked rather rhetorically, 'Andrew Thomas?' It was like he just found a long lost relative.

The other two panellists looked totally lost, wondering what was getting the old man so excited. The old man calmed himself down, looked me straight in the eyes and said: 'Andrew Thomas was from Oyo. Yes or no?' A few questions and answers later, and I was walking out of the door with an 'iou'. Worth adding that the other two panellists were drawn back into the interview only when the old man made reference to Chief Bode Thomas. Aside from the bursary award, I won something more significant that day. The realisation that the history of Andrew Thomas was sliding into extinction. My journey back to the 19th century started that day, albeit on a 'wish' level.

Oral history here and there, at times like little jigsaw pieces, put my 'time machine' on its tracks. Then followed my very first literature on Andrew Thomas – one page in Macmillan's 'The Red Book of West Africa', first published in 1920. My fascination ballooned with every additional information or material. I then realised this was not a man to be celebrated just by the extended Andrew Thomas family. This was a man the Black race should be proud of, and anyone with ambition, Black or White, can learn a thing or two from.

When the Black History Month 2007 steering group of the University of the Arts London decided to include the launch of the book in its programme, my time machine gathered momentum.

With the biography now in print, please welcome me back to the 21st century!

Kunle Thomas
October 2007

ACKNOWLEDGEMENTS

This is the toughest part for me. Where can I possibly start? Won't I need another book to tell the story of the inestimable support bestowed on me? Let me start by thanking the University of the Arts London, particularly its senior management and the Black History Month 2007 steering group. Chaired by Lorna Stewart, the group's 'extra mile' determination to ensure the success of all its activities is definitely worth a specific mention. Must give additional credit to Lorna for bravely agreeing to write the foreword at short notice. My heartfelt thanks to Dr Will Bridge (Deputy Rector, University of the Arts London) and Steve Pope (Editor, 'The Voice' newspaper) for providing quotes on the book.

I wish to also thank Dr Marion Wallace (Curator) and the rest of the dedicated staff of the British Library (including those at the Colindale newspaper section) for their guidance and support. Same appreciation goes to staff at the School of Oriental and African Studies (SOAS) library, part of the University of London. Can I possibly forget the professional support from staff at the National Archives, Kew Gardens, Surrey and those at the Nigerian National Archives at the University of Ibadan? Special thanks also to my Chief Proof Reader (I know he is too modest to accept that job title), Wole Adeniji. Much deserved respect and thanks to my creative team, including Tade Agbesanwa of Visual Edge and Kayode Olorunfemi of Effluxart and to my very lovely and dedicated Research Assistant, Funmi Olaniran. Sincere appreciation also goes to Prof. J.F. Ade-Ajayi and Dr Tunde Oduwobi, both historians.

Time to go home. I'm eternally grateful to my mum, siblings and relatives for their unflinching support and provision of useful information for this book. My brother, Dr Bode Thomas, deserves specific mention for making available to me the wealth of information and materials he has been putting together on Andrew W Thomas and children. Now, very warm, kiss-packed thanks to my two princesses, Sabrina Konyinsola and Jessica Olufunmilayo for their understanding and support, despite seeing less of daddy in the last few months. Must also give thanks to their mum, Tayo.

I say thanks with the same degree of appreciation and indebtedness to many others who supported me in one form or the other but whose names or organisations I have not mentioned. Perhaps old age is gradually catching up with me, and with that comes failing memory.

Thank you all.

ABOUT THE AUTHOR

Kunle Thomas is the Principal Consultant at Top Agenda Communications (public relations and marketing communications consultancy) and associate lecturer at the London College of Communication (LCC), University of the Arts London. He holds a postgraduate degree (MSc) in public relations from the University of Stirling, Scotland and membership of the Chartered Institute of Public Relations (MCIPR) in the UK. He commenced his communications career in 1988 at Grant Advertising Nigeria (then an affiliate of McCann Erickson), and has since worked in wide ranging sectors in the UK. Adding a different kind of 'feather to his cap', he was appointed a Churchwarden of St Luke's Church of England, Canning Town, London in April 2007.

Kunle is the youngest grandchild of Andrew W Thomas.

Kunle Thomas

The Colourful Black Auctioneer

Chapter 1

Family background and the Oyo royalty

Andrew Wilkinson Thomas was born in Oyo, western Nigeria, on 31 January 1856. The exact location of his birth was *Orupo*, a name given to bedrooms within the palace of the Alafin of Oyo, perhaps the paramount and most powerful of the Yoruba kings.[1]

His father, John Iwolode Thomas (Iwolode means 'it is you that has arrived' and could also mean 'it is you that has come back'), was a son of Alafin Abiodun who was enthroned in 1775 and ruled till his death in 1805. Born in 1795, Iwolode died at the ripe old age of 92 on 13 August 1887. Still very visible on the marble gravestone of Iwolode in Oyo is

A section of John Iwolode Thomas' gravestone, Oyo

a list of his children: Mrs Patience Heatherset, John Ayorinde, William Odunaro and, the 'baby' of the family, Andrew Durojaiye Obaleye.

Andrew Thomas later changed his name to Andrew Wilkinson Thomas and stopped the use of the names Durojaiye and Obaleye. His mum repeatedly endured the pain and sadness of quite a few infant deaths before he was born, hence the name Durojaiye (meaning: stay to enjoy life).

A child born under this kind of scenario is what the Yoruba of Nigeria call 'abiku', meaning 'born to die'. One likely reason for dropping this name may be to avoid the stigma the 'abiku' name ties, like a noose, round the neck of its bearers. Obaleye (meaning: royalty is glorious) may have been considered as drawing too much attention to his royal lineage.

Another reason for dropping his Yoruba names in favour of an English name could have been the same reason why many immigrants to the UK, US or other advanced English speaking countries tend to drop their native names in favour of an 'adopted' English name. This swap, they think, would help them get along and integrate better, particularly at work. Nigeria being under British colonial rule at the time, coupled with Andrew Thomas' years in the colonial civil service, may have possibly influenced the change of name.

Andrew Thomas' royal links had been established by previous research-

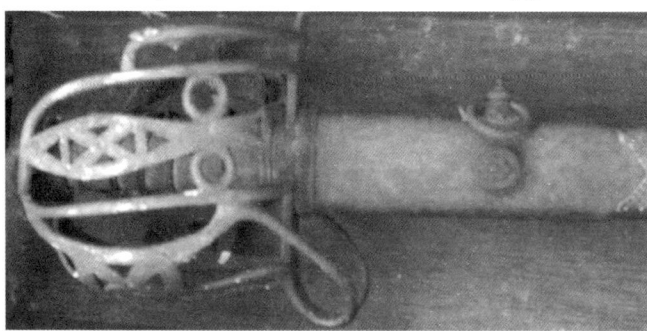

The Thomas' royal sword from the Alafin of Oyo – about a century old.

Family background and the Oyo royalty

A fuller view of the Thomas' royal sword

ers and authors, though the exact relationship not as precisely stated above. Webster (1964)[2], a Research Fellow at the Institute of African Studies, University of Ibadan, Nigeria wrote:

"A. W. Thomas ... his father was a close relative of the Alafin (the paramount ruler of the Yorubas)."

He added:

"Thomas' influence was the result of the prestige of his birth..."

Iwolode Thomas was kidnapped along with others, probably about the age of 10 (or as a young teenager), in a raid by agents of slave traders.[3]

One of such instances of kidnapping was recorded by Law (1977)

"During the reign at Oyo of Alafin Abiodun ... there was an outbreak of kidnapping ... and several Oyo traders were enslaved. Abiodun ... sent orders ... to suppress these kidnappings"[4]

En route to the Americas or England, he was rescued or released in Sierra Leone (Freetown). The release of John Iwolode was said to have been brought about by Alafin Abiodun's demand for the immediate release of his son[5]. Others that were released (or escaped) in Sierra Leone included Samuel Ajayi Crowther, the grandfather of Herbert Macaulay, a Nigerian nationalist. Another source of oral history[6] has it that the ship in which he was being transported was attacked by the Royal Navy (of Great Britain) in Sierra Leone. This would suggest this shipment of slaves to be after the abolition of slave trade by the British parliament in 1807 – two years after the death of Alafin Abiodun.

Alafin Siyanbola Onikepe Ladugbolu

Family background and the Oyo royalty

Ajayi and Iwolode became good friends and both returned to the neighbouring towns of Iseyin and Oyo respectively. Before their return, they were baptized and given two English 'faith' names each. Iwolode added John and Thomas while Ajayi 'adopted' the names Samuel and Crowther. Iwolode invited Christian missionaries to Oyo and helped establish the first church in the town, St Michael Anglican Church, Esiele. The name of the area was later changed to 'Oke Ebo' (meaning: the white man's neighbourhood) and still referred to as such till today – despite the fact that you can hardly see any Caucasian resident in the town in recent times. Iwolode's friend, Ajayi Crowther, translated the English bible to Yoruba. A few decades down the line, Andrew Thomas and Herbert Macaulay (Ajayi Crowther's grandson) continued to foster the friendship between the two families.

Andrew W Thomas belonged to the Agunloye 'ruling house' from which came Alafin Lawani, Ladugbolu (sometimes referred to as Ladigbolu) and Gbadegesin.

Andrew Thomas' primary education was in Ibadan, also in western Nigeria, and about 60 kilometres south of Oyo. It was while in Ibadan that Andrew Thomas did his baptism, one of the key tenets of the Christian faith. This symbolic 'dead to sin, new life in Christ' ceremony was performed by Rev. D Hinderer, one of the prominent Church Missionary Society (CMS) missionaries based in western Nigeria at the time. The other prominent European CMS missionary stationed in western Nigeria was Rev. Henry Townsend, and he was mostly stationed in and around Abeokuta.[7] Hinderer and Townsend were part of the Yoruba Mission of the CMS.

It is perhaps not too surprising that Andrew Thomas' early childhood was spent in Ibadan rather than his native Oyo. The Oyo royal lineage to which he belonged also had to live in Ibadan for many years.

In 1875, Adeyemi and Lawani contested the symbolic 'royal stool', with the former declared victorious. The belief at the time was that the unsuccessful candidate would be better off going into voluntary exile while the victorious candidate rules. In line with this tradition, Lawani, and his little son Ladugbolu, left Oyo and settled in Ibadan for 30 years - from 1875 to 1905. Lawani returned to Oyo to ascend the throne on the death of Alafin Adeyemi.

Andrew Thomas left Ibadan for Lagos, the 'seat' of the British colonial government, to commence his secondary school education. Just before we retrace the steps of Andrew Thomas as he embarks on his journey to Lagos, let us look at a major development that altered the balance of power among key Yoruba towns, particularly Oyo and Ibadan.

In February 1893, the British colonial government, through the Administrator of Lagos, Captain G C Denton, entered into a treaty with the Alafin of Oyo. More clearly than the two treaties before it (1886, 1888), the 1893 treaty sets out the limitations of the king and therefore vested a sort of 'Ombudsman' status in the colonial government. The treaty gave the latter the final 'word' in the arbitration of disputes in Oyo and the wider Yoruba kingdom, where British subjects were involved. This, in effect, usurped the centuries' old power of the Alafin which his subjects reiterate in their everyday salutations:

'Iku babayeye, igbakeji orisa'

MEANING:

'Fearsome as death, the next in command to the gods'

The treaty also forbade the king from entering into any arrangement with any other foreign government or their representatives, an obvious move to maintain a monopolistic stranglehold over the ancient and very important region.

Next stop, Ibadan. In August 1893, it was Ibadan's turn to put pen to paper (or was it poisoned chalice to the throat?). One of the key points

Family background and the Oyo royalty

Captain William Alston Ross (District Commissioner, Oyo)

in the treaty with Ibadan was the stationing of a British Resident Officer, backed by soldiers, in Ibadan. With little or no room for negotiation, the Bale (king) of Ibadan signed the treaty reluctantly. With its vast diplomatic experience, the British colonial government had a carrot tied to the stick. Not surprising that the very first section of the treaty states:

"That the general administration of the internal affairs of the following towns ….and in all the countries … is vested in the general government of Ibadan … notwithstanding that the Alafin is recognised as the King and Head of Yoruba-land."

There were reasons to suggest that the Alafin also signed the February 1893 treaty without full understanding of its ramifications.

That was the political situation inherited by Alafin Lawani and his heir to the throne, Ladugbolu. But all that was about to change with one event

– the appointment of Captain William Alston Ross as the first District Commissioner for Oyo, effective 1 May 1906. Ross established a legacy that outlived its quarter of a century stay in Oyo. For the Alafin and the senior chiefs, Ross was like the biblical 'manna from heaven', the white knight in shining armour who galloped to Oyo's rescue, to deliver it from the political ignominy spitted out by the 1893 treaties. To the ordinary native and the junior chiefs, he was the Satan incarnate, a choking nightmare for the cursed.

Let's see why, in the first instance, Ross would want to reinstate Oyo to its past glory and political power. We will then look at the 'carrot' he mercilessly chewed on in return.

Three years prior to Ross taking his post in Oyo, there was a government policy dictated in 1903 by the Governor of Lagos, Sir William MacGregor. He wanted:

"The authority of the Alafin ... extended beyond its present limits, over districts ruled by him and his predecessors"

It was therefore a primary remit of Ross to implement this policy. In addition to the policy issue, there was good cordiality between Ross and Alafin Lawani and the Crown Prince, particularly with the latter. Ross and Prince Ladugbolu were in the same age bracket, so it was relatively easier for them to get along well. Having lived in Ibadan for 30 years and experienced first hand the power disparity between Oyo and Ibadan, the king pledged loyalty to the British colonial government and sought Ross' help in ensuring Oyo was returned to its former status and glory.[8]

Ross obliged the wishes of the king and Prince Ladugbolu, and the Alafin of Oyo was once again the paramount ruler of the Yorubas. But at what price?

Ross became power intoxicated. He realised the need to learn Yoruba language and understand the culture. For an European, he did that to a commendable level. However, the use to which he put his knowledge and power had an ugly stink to it. He was known to have regularly said:

Alafin, pataki.

Ross, pataki

MEANING:

King of Oyo, very important personality

Ross, very important personality

Ross was also known to be heavy handed and brutal with natives who walked past him without prostrating and rolling on the ground to greet him, a traditional greeting normally reserved for the king.

In January 1914, the Ibadan chiefs challenged Ross' demand that they, with the exception of the Bale, should prostrate for him. They reported the matter to Governor–General Federick Luggard. However, not much came out of this case as H Childs, one of the officers involved in investigating the matter opined:

"….prostration was a normal way in Yorubaland of showing respect … it was not infrequently seen in the streets."[9]

Ross' power intoxication was not confined to his desire to see people prostrate on the ground for him. He also seemed to enjoy slapping people, though had his native aide do this on most occasions for the flimsiest excuse. If, for example, a native walked past him without prostrating, Ross would impolitely stop the person and communicate in a coded language to his native aide whose name was Ogundele:

Ogundele, fi mi han

MEANING:

Ogundele, reveal my identity

Ordinarily, one may expect Ogundele to formally introduce Ross. But what usually followed was the sound of a heavy slap on the face of the unsuspecting native, synchronised with:

Iwo, Ross ni yi

MEANING:

Eh, you, this is Ross.

I wonder what the insulting beckoning of the native would be like if Ogundele was from East London and spoke only cockney. The slap would ring along with:

Oi, meet my gov, Ross

Indulge me just once more. Let's see what Jamaican patois (pidgin English) would sound like, along with the slap, in making this introduction:

Yo, dat a Ross.

There was an incident in Lagos that had the hallmarks of Ross' excessiveness. Mr Douglas, an officer in the Lagos colonial administration, confessed that he "cuffed" (punched or slapped) a native junior colleague, the excuse being that he was "provoked". [10] This matter was reported in 1914 by a newspaper, 'Times of Nigeria' to the Governor–General and the news even reached the Secretary of State for the Colonies, the Right Honourable Lewis Harcourt. His punishment? He was officially reprimanded and warned that the matter could affect his chances of promotion. I wonder what signal the matter and its handling gave to someone like Ross: 'Carry on slapping' or 'put on the brakes or you would be heading for a crash'. What do you think? The reality was that the slapping subculture did not fade away.

One other salutation used by the natives that conveyed Ross' brutality was:

Family background and the Oyo royalty

'Onisokoto pempe tin se elewu etu riyariya'

MEANING:

The man in shorts (Ross usually wore shorts) who orders the man in expensive fabrics about and causes him to be disoriented.

Ross' first step on Nigerian soil was on 13 January 1903. 13th? No wonder!

Andrew Thomas attended CMS Grammar school, Lagos. Founded on 6 June 1859, it was the country's first secondary grammar school, and for decades remained the only secondary grammar school for boys.

The Principal (Head Teacher) of the school at the time of Andrew Thomas was Rev. Thomas Babington Macaulay (father of one of Nigeria's Nationalists, Herbert Heelas Macaulay). He was Head Teacher for 20 years, from the school's inception in 1859 (with only six students) to the time of his death in 1879. The school was then located in a storey building, 'Cotton House', on Broad Street. It held the enviable position that I call the 'Lagos Oxbridge', and the school was the hunting ground for recruiters of labour, particularly the British colonial administration. One of such 'Old Boys' was Henry Carr who joined the colonial administration and later became the country's first indigenous Inspector of Schools.[11]

The school motto, since it was set up in 1859, remains:

'Nisi Dominus Frustra'

MEANING:

'Without God, we labour in vain"

The motto, taken from the biblical injunction in Psalm 127, moulded the school's tradition and values.

It is fair to say that the values inculcated into students at CMS Grammar School Lagos, complemented Andrew Thomas' Christian upbringing and baptism. The combination of these factors must have influenced his adult life, including the major role he played in the church.

Chapter 2

Last with lasting legacy – meet Chief Bode Thomas and siblings

Tell me the number of children you have and I will tell you how important and wealthy you are. That was a traditional mindset of many Africans that may not have completely vanished even today. The two sides of the 'equation' were believed to be directly proportional – the more the children, the more the wealth and prestige. This school of thought may have influenced Andrew Thomas' propensity to procreate. He went for the first... then the second. He proceeded... 3... 4... 5... 6... 10. Have a break. Ready? 11... 12... 13. In all, 13 children comprising of seven daughters and six sons.

One other factor that may have contributed to having many children was his desire for a male child. The first four children were all female. So

Chief Bode Thomas

he forged ahead. Without further ado, let me introduce you to another 'baby' of the family, the youngest of Andrew Thomas' children – Chief Bode Thomas.

Though the last child, Chief Bode Thomas was arguably the most popular among Andrew Thomas' children in today's generation. Major roads, school, hospital plaque and even a ship still bear his name for posterity.

Chief Akanbi Olabode Thomas was born in 1920 in Lagos, Nigeria. Like his father, he attended CMS Grammar School, Lagos. Unlike the days of his father when it was CMS Grammar School or no school, there were options but CMS Grammar school remained the family's favourite. On the completion of his secondary school education in 1937, he was employed in a clerical role at the Nigerian Railway where he earned a daily wage of two shillings.[12]

Next stop; London. Records from the Middle Temple archive reveals:

"On 23 October 1939 Akanbi Olabode Thomas of 85 Odunfa Street, Lagos, aged 19 years, last son of Andrew Wilkinson Thomas of 85 Odunfa Street, Lagos, auctioneer, was admitted to the Middle Temple. He was called to the Bar here on 17th June 1942."[13]

The desire or need to stay behind in London after qualifying as a barrister was not on Bode's card. Then the youngest Nigerian barrister, Bode practiced law on his own for a brief period before teaming up with two equally dynamic lawyers to form a new law chambers. The two men were Chief Remi Fani-Kayode and Chief Frederick Rotimi Williams, and the chambers was called Thomas, Williams and Kayode.

The law chambers soon gained a reputation for brilliance and professionalism and was in the top bracket of indigenous law firms in the country. Many young Nigerian lawyers benefited from the experience of these three partners. One of such lawyers was Chief Sobo Sowemimo,

Last with lasting legacy - meet Chief Bode Thomas and siblings

From left to right: Chief Bode Thomas, Sir Ahmadu Bello (the Sardauna of Sokoto) and Sir Abubakar Tafawa Balewa (later became the first Prime Minister of independent Nigeria).

The Colourful Black Auctioneer

Chief Obafemi Awolowo
Leader, Action Group (political party)

Typical dressing of a Yoruba War General

SAN,[14] who died in September 2007 at the age of 81. Not long after the enviable reputation of the law practice was firmly rooted, Bode set himself another target which the law practice could not deliver. He believed Nigerians should rule Nigeria, and he wanted to contribute to making that dream a reality. He therefore put aside his 'wig and gown' in exchange for *agbada*, the traditional Yoruba 'gown' which has come to symbolise a career in politics.

The seed of nationalism was already sown in Bode while a law student in London. Immediately after returning to Nigeria in 1942, he joined the Nigerian Youth Movement (NYM). The NYM was a political breeding ground for young intellectuals and professionals. Together with the NCNC (National Council of Nigeria and the Cameroons) led by Dr Nnamdi Azikwe, the NYM began the long journey that would eventually dish out P45s (a UK document issued to those who just lost their jobs) to the British colonial government and its administrators in Nigeria. Realising that the political objectives he set himself may not be

The Colourful Black Auctioneer

Chief Andrew Olatunji Thomas

realised through the NYM and its alliances, he left in 1950. But it was a comma, not a full stop in his political career. In March 1951, he teamed up with another lawyer, Chief Obafemi Awolowo, to form the Action Group (AG). It was on the platform of the AG that Bode got elected into the Western Region House of Assembly in the 1951 elections. He was soon nominated, alongside three others, for membership of the national legislature. Bode's rise through the political ladder was phenomenal. No sooner did he get to the national legislature was he made Minister of Transport.

The ministerial role was a means to an end for Bode. So, it was not too surprising that he was willing to give up this enviable post in just two years. Why? He was one of the key proponents of a Bill calling for the end of British rule in 1956. The Bill, officially proposed by Anthony Enahoro (an AG colleague) was moved with the support of NCNC ministers. However, the effort of Bode and others was thwarted by the coalition of the four northern Nigerian ministers with the six British officials in the National Legislative Council. Bode was not alone in his resignation protest; his fellow AG ministers as well as the NCNC ministers also resigned over this issue.

His exit from the inner sanctuary of political power was very short lived. His dynamism, oratory and professionalism were needed where they mattered most. Later in the same year, 1953, he got another ministerial post – Minister of Works. He held this post until his life sadly ended on 20 November 1953 at the very tender age of 33.

The biography of Bode Thomas, no matter how short, would be grossly incomplete without more reference to his native Oyo. In recognition of his achievements and potential, the King of Oyo, Alafin Adeniran Adeyemi II, conferred on him one of the highest chieftaincy titles of the land, Balogun (the War General) of Oyo. In 'days' way before his time, Chief Bode Thomas would have had to command the Oyo army. The army's armoury would probably include sakabula (dane guns) and ogun (charms).

The charms, used in conjunction with ofo (incantations), could – as often claimed - turn an approaching enemy army against itself. I often wonder how Captain Ross got away with all his atrocities without experiencing the charms first hand. He should also have asked his friend, Alafin Ladugbolu for some of the charms which the British and the Allied Forces could have used against Germany. But would it really work against ballistic missiles, bombs and machine guns. Hmm. Good question. You never know until you try!

I very much doubt Chief Bode Thomas would have been able to cope with the tasks of a generalissimo. Don't think that was part of the curriculum at CMS Grammar School, Lagos or the barrister training at Middle Temple Inn, London.

The circumstances leading to his death still remained shrouded in mystery, speculations and conspiracy theories on the scale that seemed to rival that of the assassination of President Kennedy of USA. His life reminds me of Elton John's song 'Candle in the Wind' recorded in memory of Diana, Princess of Wales. The 'candle' of Chief Bode Thomas must have been burning at both ends. His life was very short, but my God, how bright! Even now, while writing this biography, tear drops kissed randomly selected letters on my keyboard. It's hard not to imagine what would have been.

Chief Bode Thomas was survived by six children, including Abimbola Bode-Thomas (hotelier), Mrs Eniola Fadayomi (lawyer, entrepreneur, former AfriBank Chair and former Lagos State Attorney General & Commissioner for Justice), Tokunbo Thomas, SAN and Dupe Bode-Thomas (educationist). Others were Dapo Bode-Thomas (former member of Lagos State House of Assembly and more recently Special Adviser to Lagos State Governor on chieftaincy affairs) and Afolami

Last with lasting legacy - meet Chief Bode Thomas and siblings

Mrs Comfort Gbadero Agbe

Thomas, both deceased.

Let us now turn our attention to the siblings of Chief Bode Thomas, though not in any particular order.

Chief Andrew Olatunji Thomas was born in 1900. He was a lawyer who was revered all over the old western region of Nigeria for his handling of criminal cases. Like Chief Bode Thomas, he trained in London as a barrister. Sir Louis Mbanefo (knighted in 1961 when he was Chief Justice of Eastern Nigeria) publicly commented that Chief Andrew Olatunji Thomas was one of the legal giants Nigeria once had. Again like Chief Bode, he was honoured with a chieftaincy title by the king of Oyo,

Mrs Adenike Gamra

Alafin Adeniran Adeyemi II. His title was Ona Aka of Oyo. This was a particularly special title as it means 'the grandfather to the king' and was reserved for royalty. Chief A O Thomas was one of the key people that helped change the custom that required the Aremo (crown prince) to leave Oyo if a king from another royal lineage was enthroned after the death of the Aremo's father. When he retired from active law practice, he was made a Judge of the Customary Court.

He, together with his younger brother Chief Bode Thomas, further enhanced the status of Andrew Thomas and the family as a whole. It was probably the first time in Nigeria that a family had two brothers in both regional houses of parliament (Chief Bode in the House of Assembly and Chief Olatunji in the House of Chiefs).

Chief Olatunji Thomas was very popular for his elaborate parties and generally active social life, just as much as he was well known for his mastery of criminal law. One of such celebrations was the Aremo festival at the family's royal farm, Olufon, in Oyo. He added colour, in bucketfuls, to this key festival and invited dignitaries from far and wide – including many Europeans – to the celebration.

Tinuola Babatunde Thomas

He died on 23 December 1973. Though he had three children, he was survived by a son, Tunde Thomas. Now deceased, Tunde recounted the pampering and generosity lavished on him by Alafin Gbadegesin on his return to Oyo after years of living in the UK.[15]

The Colourful Black Auctioneer

Jacob Omosalewa Thomas, born 23 June 1887, was a surveyor turned auctioneer. Like his dad and brothers, his secondary school education was at CMS Grammar School, Lagos. He trained as a surveyor at Federal School of Survey, near Oyo, West Africa's oldest surveying school. He was popularly called *baba onigbanjo*, a reference to his auctioneering profession. He enjoyed playing musical instruments, including piano and violin. He died on 7 May 1963, aged 76. Among his many children … wait for it … about 30! .... are Justice Omololu Thomas (retired Judge and currently the oldest grandchild of Andrew Thomas … in his 80's), Dr Oloyede Thomas (pharmacologist and pharmacist), Oyinda Thomas and Oyekan Thomas who left his mortgage/financial consultancy in the UK for farming in Oyo.[16]

Born on 18 May 1890, **Mrs Comfort Gbadero Agbe** was a seamstress (or should we say a fashion designer?) and interior decorator who could count the Nigeria Railways as one of her clients. She was a very active member of St Jude's Church, Ebute-Metta, Lagos where she was credited

Mrs Ayodele Coker

for popularising the 'triumphant' horse riding as a celebration of Easter Sunday and so nicknamed 'mama magesinlo'. She loved gardening. She volunteered to look after the church garden and regularly decorated the church with fresh flowers in readiness for church services and major events. Mrs Agbe died on 17 May 1974, on the eve of her 84th birthday. Among her children is Bisi Agbe.[17]

Mary Adenike Gamra was born on 25 May 1915. Starting off as a dress maker (yes, you guessed right - fashion designer), she later moved into textile trading and haulage. Her textile trading focused on the importation of quality lace materials from Italy while her haulage business dealt primarily with the transportation of building materials.

Nike, as she was called (could this be the origin of the famous sport merchandise brand? Naaaaa. That's Adenike for short), was a devout Christian, but not of the African Church or the Anglican Church genres that characterised her family upbringing. She did it her way, the third way, and headed for the Pope's flock. Her decision to be a Catholic was however not unpredictable. Her attendance of Mount Carmel Convent School, Ebute-Metta, Lagos had a little glue which bonded her to Catholicism. She regularly attended St Dominic's Church, Yaba, Lagos and was a member of the Legion of Mary, an international Catholic organisation, from about 1956 till her death, four decades later. Her main hobbies were gardening and flower arrangement (just like her sister, Mrs Agbe), as well as cake baking and decoration.

Now, imagine you were comfortably seated at a wedding reception, waiting to hear the juicy bit about how the couple met. Well, you're in luck! Nike occasionally visited her brother, Tinuola, in Ile-Ife where he was working at the time. Then the visits grew from occasional to regular, and then to regularly frequent. Yes, she loved her brother, but her brother's good friend caught her attention. Mr. C. S. Gamra, originally from Lebanon, you may come out from behind the curtains! Nothing else to add, except that Adenike became Mrs. Gamra in 1945 and had two sons – Joseph and Victor. Captain Joseph Gamra is today one of Nigeria's most experienced commercial pilots and his brother Victor – well, let me address him properly – Col. Victor Gamra (retired), formerly of the Nigerian Army Military Police Corps. Mrs Nike Gamra died on 26 February 2004.[18]

Tinuola Thomas was born in Lagos on 29th April 1917. Like his brothers, he attended CMS Grammar School, Lagos and benefited from the guidance and tutorship of Rev (Dr) Olumide Lucas with whom he and young Bode lived for some time. He also did a short course in marketing at Yaba College of Technology.

Highlights of his employment history included work at Zik Press, the law chambers co-founded by his brother, Thomas, Williams and Kayode and the Western Nigeria Development Corporation (WNDC). His knowledge of law pertaining to real estate gained him his last job – membership of the Lagos State Rent Tribunal, Ministry of Justice. He was the land law luminary that never was!

He was an active member of the Men's Bible Class, Cathedral Church of Christ, Lagos. He was also a keen sportsman, notably tennis and table tennis. His dancing skill won him a trophy at a competition, understandably with a little help from the ikoto footwork of his wife and dancing partner, Mrs Olabisi Thomas. They were married for 61 years, a true case of 'till death do us part'.

Tinuola's death on 18 May 2007, about three weeks after his 90th birthday celebration, marked the end of a generation as he was the last surviving child of Andrew Thomas. Among his 10 children are Tunde Thomas (marketing communications professional and former adviser to a government minister), Dr Bode Thomas (vet surgeon), Diran Thomas (Deputy Head of a Lagos state secondary school) and Kunle Thomas (PR/marketing communications consultant, associate lecturer and author of this biography). Others include Olamide Thomas, Mrs Oyinkan Obasi, Disun Thomas and Olakunle Thomas. Two are now deceased - Kolawole Thomas and Olayiwola Thomas.

Mrs Christiana Ayodele Coker was the first child of Andrew W Thomas. Referring to Mrs Coker, Chief Bode Thomas and Chief Andrew Olatunji Thomas, Webster (1964) commented on Andrew Thomas:

> "He educated two of his sons as lawyers. His daughter married one of the wealthiest men of Lagos."

Mrs Coker's children included Chief Ladugbolu Coker, a UK trained aeronautics engineer and one of the first indigenes to be on the management board of Nigeria Airways. His brother, Gbadebo Coker was also an accomplished automobile engineer. Though grandchildren of Andrew Thomas, they were both older than a few of Andrew Thomas' children - including my father, Tinuola Thomas.[19]

Mrs Coker, probably for being the eldest, was the only child named in the will of Andrew Thomas as one of the trustees of his vast estate. She died in 1948, aged over 70.

The other children of Andrew Thomas were Mrs Victoria Ashinyanbi Taylor (nicknamed 'anti alakoro', after her area of residence), Mrs Yetunde Macarthy, Mrs Naomi Olayinka West, Mrs Sarah Omodunni Adekoye, Mr Oladipo Thomas and Mr Bankole Thomas.

Chapter 3

Trust me; you don't want to see Andy

It would be interesting to know what his last day at CMS Grammar School, Lagos, was like. What was on his mind? Had he planned the next few years of his life – what to do, when where and how? Or was he just hoping and waiting for a good opportunity to show its beautiful head? If his last day at secondary school was anything like mine, then he would be exchanging contact details with fellow students, moving his bags and baggage from the dormitory and generally feeling happy and sad at the same time.

What we do know was that his next move was into the labour market. His first job was a clerical position at Campbell and Co, general merchants based in Lagos. It was from this job that he joined the British colonial government. The Lagos-based civil service job was also a clerical position, at least as a starting point. But where did that lead him – steps to the

Sir Hawley John Glover
Administrator and Governor of Lagos Colony

mountain or slides to the valley?

The very limited literature available on Andrew Thomas indicated that he ascended the steps of promotion in the civil service, rising to the post of Deputy Registrar of the Supreme Court. What a proud grandchild that made me. So when I got to that stage of his life in my research, I blended into the rusty brown, rustling, dusty pages of archival materials. It was like being in a time machine.

The Colonial Office List was the little capsule in which I zzzzeee'd back to the second half of the 19th century. 1860s. Andrew W Thomas! No answer. So I pressed the button … oh my God! 1880. That was the ultra-superfastforward button. I had to go back a bit. This time, slowly. 1879 … 78 … 70. Andrew Thomas! Faint answer. I looked, excited, my heart struggling to equal the speed of my time capsule. It was very close, but my search was far from eureka.

Sir Alfred Moloney K.C.M.G
Governor of Lagos Colony (1886, 1887, 1890)

M M Thomas – Charge Clerk (Constabulary, Lagos) - 1878, 79 and 1880.

And, interestingly:

A. W Thompson – Deputy Registrar (Judicial Department, Gold Coast) - 1878

Now, I can empathise with earlier researchers and authors. I took a little break in my little machine, and …yes, had a Kit Kat![20] Let's try a little exercise, a play with words. Take out the 'offending' three letters from the name (Thompson) and you'd get p, o, n. Now, change the 'o' to a 'u'. So, I concluded that pon is a play on names, just as pun is a play on words!

I was disappointed but determined to forge ahead. I hit the 'very slow' button of my time capsule and was crawling through 1881, 82, 82, 82… I'm stuck. Andrew W Thomas! The capsule shook, as if a raft had been hit by a Tsunami.[21] I calmed my head and looked. And there he was, sitting quietly on the dusty brown paper:

Capt. George C. Denton
Administrator, Lagos Colony (1889, '90, '93, '95, '96, 1900)

A. W. Thomas – Charge Clerk (Constabulary) - £50 per annum

I wiped my face with my perspiring palm. I wasn't seeing things. Eureka!

The few seconds of elation was quickly followed by a gut-wrenching feeling of disappointment. I went out looking for Deputy Registrar of the Supreme Court and had to settle for a Charge Clerk? That's life!

So how much money did civil service jobs command in late 19th century Nigeria? Let's look at a few 1882 examples:

Job Title	Department	Annual Salary
Registrar of the Supreme Court	Judicial	£200
Deputy Registrar of the Supreme Court	Judicial	£100
Crown Prosecutor	Judicial	£100
Superintendent of Police	Constabulary	£150
Schoolmaster	Constabulary	£36
Bailiff	Judicial	£40
Messenger	Judicial	£24

Extract from the 'Colonial Office List' (Lagos colony, 1882)

Considering that the pounds sterling earned by the civil servants in Nigeria at the time was just as strong in value as the British pounds, let's think of how far £50 will go in today's UK economy. Will be ok for food and drinks for two at an averagely priced restaurant. Money paid, till closed. That's it for the next 12 months. A visit to my local ASDA or TESCO will probably gulp £100 or more for a week's family shopping. What about the messenger on £2 per month? Would be interesting to know how much he/she would set aside for food, transportation, clothing, etc. But of course the value of money at that time cannot be compared to the purchasing power of today's money.

**Court House/Registrar's Office
Tinubu Square, Lagos**

Let me draw your attention to a small, perhaps not too important detail about Andrew Thomas' civil service days. There was an entry in the Government Gazette which caught my attention. It was dated 31 January 1887 and posted by H. Iiggins, Acting Colonial Secretary. It reads:

"Jan 10: Mr Andrew W. Thomas, Charge clerk, in the Lagos Constabulary granted 3 months leave of absence on full pay to enable him to visit Oyo on urgent private affairs from to-day"

If I was living in Lagos at that time, thinking whether or not to join the colonial civil service, that Gazette entry would pull me in like metal to magnet. What a compassionate, family friendly employer? Donning my

Public relations[22] cap, I would see it as using every available opportunity to create a good corporate image for the colonial government.

If '3 months leave on full pay' was a PR stunt, why the detail of exactly where he was going? Ah ha! Could that be the 'call to action' to all voluntary and commissioned 007s?[23] Imagine what would happen if he was then found in a beer parlour (pub) somewhere in Lagos, when he should be in Oyo, guzzling down a few bottles and tapping his feet to …. my God, who were the African musicians of … the Ebenezer Obe, Sunny Ade, Fela Kuti, Nico Nbanga, Victor Uwaifo… of that era? I don't think there is any 'warning label' restriction to developing conspiracy theories, yet! As noted in chapter 1, his father - Iwolode Thomas - died in August 1887. So maybe his father was ill for some time before his death, and he had to visit and care for him.

Andrew Thomas remained a Charge Clerk for about seven years. During those years, he served on many occasions as a juror, a role that outlived his civil service employment.

So, in those days, you're better off staying far away from Andrew Thomas. Go have fun, go read, go work. Whatever you do, you really don't want to see Andrew Thomas. An appointment with the Charge Clerk smells rat.

On 1 January 1889, Andrew Thomas kissed his job goodbye after seven years and immediately launched his new auctioneering career. At the time of his resignation, his annual salary had increased from £50 to … have a guess …. £60. What a rise!

Chapter 4

The auctioneer is born

The year 1891 must have been brightly highlighted by Andrew Thomas. Inscribed on his mind and in his brain. It had to be the 'all change' year, the year marking a new beginning, a change of direction. I suspect he must have been in the 'I have a dream' mood a year or two prior. If he had the dream of a very successful career, wealth, mansion, influence … he wasn't going to allow anything to rudely wake him up to the reality of his current position. It wouldn't matter if he was the Registrar of the Supreme Court or the messenger. He had a dream, and he had to wake up, gloves in hand, to shovel his dream into reality.

He resigned from his civil service job as Charge Clerk on 1 January 1891, and woke up the following morning as a licensed auctioneer. For a New Year resolution, take that! His auctioneer's licence, dated 2 January 1891, was published alongside four others (including one auctioneers agent's licence) in the Government Gazette.[24]

Andrew Thomas' bold career move reminds me of the words of Theodore Roosevelt, Jr. who served as the 26th US president from 14 September 1901 – 4 March 1909. He was quoted as saying:

"Far better it is to dare mighty things, to win glorious triumphs, even though checkered by failure, than to rank with those poor souls who neither enjoy much nor suffer much because they live in the grey twilight that knows neither victory nor defeat."[25]

I now realise that I shouldn't have 'remortgaged' my eureka moment when I found the 1882 'Charge Clerk' entry for Andrew W Thomas. Knowing what we now know, and soon to know more of, I personally feel more respect and regard for him. Surely, if moving from the position of Chief Executive of a multinational company to becoming Chief Executive of your own company was a smart and bold move, it would certainly be a smarter and bolder move for an Administration Officer who had done intensive 'home work' to venture into the world of self

24			Government Gazette.				
49	Return of Auctioneers Licenses issued at Lagos, for the Year, 1891, under Ordinance No. 2 dated 17th January, 1878.						
No. of License.	Date of		To whom issued		Description of License	Amount paid	Remarks
	Issue	Expiry	Name	Address			
1	30th Dec. 1890.	31st Dec. 1891.	J. P. L. Davies	Broad Street	With privilege of Agents.	26 10 0	
2	31st "	"	J.P. Haastrup & son	do	"	26 10 0	
3	" "	"	Alfred Williams	Victoria Road	"	26 10 0	
1	2nd Jan. 1891.	"	A. W. Thomas & Co.	Oke Popo	Without privilege of Agents.	24 0 0	
			AUCTIONEERS AGENT'S LICENSE				
1	30th Dec.1890	31st Dec. 1891	S Sogunro Davies	Broad St,	Agents	2 0 0	
						£105 10 0	

Customs House,
Lagos, 31st January, 1891.

W. J. P. ELLIOTT,
Acting Collector of Customs.

Andrew Thomas' license – 2 January 1891

employment.

His auctioneer's licence was described as being "without privilege of Agents" and cost £24.00. So he paid exactly 40% of his enhanced annual salary of £60 to earn himself a new career direction. As shown in the table below, the total amount in the purse of the Collector of Customs for issuing the five licences was £105.10. 0 (i.e. 105 pounds, 10 shillings and zero pence), though my basic arithmetic indicates a total of £104.30.10. So, either there was a miscellaneous payment of £0.80 not shown or just an arithmetical error. Maybe I should rethink my career path and consider being an auditor? Don't think so.

In his book, Macmillan (1920)[24] wrote concerning Andrew Thomas' move into auctioneering:

"…resigning accordingly, he launched out as an auctioneer. In doing so he chose a profession for which he was peculiarly fitted."

Macmillan went further to say:

"The success which has followed Mr. Thomas in his auctioneering operations has been truly remarkable. This has undoubtedly been due to his engaging personality, his unerring judgement of the psychological and other influences that contribute to the bidding at auction sales."

Perhaps the biggest of Andrew Thomas' auctioneering projects, in terms of profile, magnitude and money, was his appointment by the British colonial government in Nigeria to auction all German assets in Nigeria and the Cameroons. This project was part of a global strategy adopted by the British and Allied Forces in a bid to weaken Germany during the First World War.

A number of previous researchers and authors acknowledged the role of Andrew Thomas in this First World War 'behind the scene' strategy.

Webster (1964) had this to say about the project:

"…he won the auction contract to dispose of the German assets from the Cameroons."

Macmillan wrote:

"On him devolved, on behalf of the Government, the sale of the German interests in Nigeria during the war, and in connection with that important work he travelled extensively throughout the Eastern and Western Provinces"

Nigeria being a British colony at the time, how much assets could Germany possibly have to warrant such a move by British and Allied Forces?

The auctioneer is born

There were up to 19 German and Austro-Hungarian companies in Nigeria at the beginning of the First World War. Of these, five were major German businesses. The epitome of German commercial enterprise in Nigeria was G L Gaiser which dominated the Lagos import and export trade, particularly the latter.

It is fair to assert that while Britain had political control of Nigeria since the middle of the 19th century, Germany weighed up heavier in the commercial arena. In fact, William Oswald & Company, a German firm that may be seen as the predecessor to G L Gaiser, was well established in Lagos prior to the city becoming a British colony.

Other active German firms in Nigeria before the outbreak of the war included Witt and Busch, a key rival to British firms since 1877. Pagenstecher & Company and the German Niger-Benue Transport Company were other examples.

In 1913, Germany was responsible for exporting about 80% of Nigeria's palm kernels, and about 50% of all exports. Also, 50% of Nigeria's untanned hides and skins and groundnut, as well as over 12% share of palm oil were exported by German businesses, particularly those from Hamburg. The Germans were also believed to be very fast and efficient in the delivery of goods, making even some British firms to prefer their shipping service.[27]

Imported articles in which German businesses traded included stockfish, twine Fez caps, 'dane guns' and gunpowder. They also had a monopoly of the supply of cutlasses which was very popular for agricultural purposes as well as copper rods. Very important on the list of German trading items were spirits and rum, the latter produced from ordinary potato and then flavoured before being cruised to Nigerian shores.

So, when World War One broke out on 14 August 1914, allowing the German flourishing commercial activities in Nigeria to continue would be tantamount to boosting the enemy's 'fire power'. Exactly one month and one week after the war commenced i.e. on 21 September 1914, Nigeria's Deputy Governor, A G Boyle stopped all Germans from trading in Nigeria. Though the Germans trading right was reintroduced a week later by the Colonial Office – to forestall what would have been a catastrophic economic stagnation – their movements and trading were under strict surveillance and restriction. For example, a 9pm curfew was introduced. They had to report daily at police stations and they were not allowed to send money to Germany. These restrictions were legitimised by the Aliens Restriction Order and Enemy Firms Liquidation Act.

Eventually, on 7 November 1914, Germany's commercial 'crown' in Nigeria was forcibly removed and trampled under foot. Germans were immediately rounded up and made prisoners of war. Their properties, including land, buildings and various merchandise were seized at various locations throughout Nigeria and the Cameroons.

The above development therefore set the stage for the appointment of Andrew W Thomas by the colonial government in Nigeria to auction all assets of Germans in Nigeria and the Cameroons. The Charge Clerk of the 1880s and 1890 had grown to arguably the leading auctioneer considered 'fit for purpose' for such a gigantic project.

Who were the key colonial government officials Andrew Thomas had to work with on the sale/auction of 'enemy' assets? The Receiver in charge was Thomas F Burrowes, who was the Comptroller of Customs. The other official Andrew Thomas would have worked with, albeit for a short time, was Mr G W Sparrow. Given the title of Assistant Receiver, Mr Sparrow's appointment was confirmed in a letter from the Crown Agents for the Colonies, dated 17 June 1915. Two days later, Mr Sparrows sailed for Lagos from England.

The auctioneer is born

Commenting on the project, Mr Sparrows said:

"I found it very voluminous (work) and I do not think it possible for the work to be completed within 12 months, more especially as Mr Tennyson (at the Colonial Office, England) made the remark that they might require me to proceed to the Cameroons after dealing with Nigeria and Sierra Leone." [26]

On 9 July 1915, Mr Sparrow resigned his appointment on health grounds. The resignation was backed by a health certificate issued by Dr H Solomon.

In December 1914, T F Burrowes placed different public notices in 'The Nigerian Gazette' advertising the sale of German goods. The common 'thread' that runs through the different ads was:

"Notice is hereby given to the public that Mr A. W Thomas, licensed auctioneer, will sell on behalf of the Receiver, by public auction ….the loose stocks and personal effects of …."

Similar notices were placed for the auction of "loose stocks and personal effects" of other German businesses such as Ring & Company.

The news of the auction plans reached Germany, and they tried to halt the plans by threats. A previously confidential memo dated 21 July 1916, drawn up in the UK Foreign Office for cabinet consideration had a response for Germany's threat. The memo was based on intelligence shared by the US, and it suggests that "local authorities in Nigeria" were planning to auction all German real estate.

The German government said if this plan was proceeded with, the property of Sir Francis Oppenheimer, referred to as His Majesty's Consul General at Frankfurt (was actually the Commercial Attaché and acting Counsellor to his Majesty's Embassy in Berlin, and residing at his own house in Frankfurt) would be seized. While the British Government communicated with the colonial government in Nigeria, it warned Germany that properties of the German Ambassador and those of other senior officials of its embassy would be confiscated if Germany's threat was carried out.

Another issue for the British government on the auction of German assets was to ensure that the assets do not revert back to the German owners. So, in addition to requiring that purchasers must be of "British or Allied nationality", the possibility of subsequently transferring the assets back to the "enemy" was blocked. The Secretary of the Manchester Chamber of Commerce wrote to the Rt. Hon. A Bonar Law MP, H M Principal Secretary of State for the Colonies:

"… and as a result of a conference at the Liverpool Chamber on the 2nd August, with Mr T. F Burrowes, the Liquidator of Enemy Property for Nigeria, a letter was addressed to him recommending that in order to ensure that the properties for sale should not ultimately be acquired by German firms, the purchasers should be debarred from transferring their interests, except to buyers who should be approved of specifically by the Nigerian Government".[29]

Was there a figure that sums up the approximate financial worth of the German assets? Some light was shed on this by Lord Lugard, the Governor–General of Nigeria in his correspondence with the Secretary of State for the Colonies:

"The transactions are very extensive and stocks will realise over £100,000 there are also large landed interests to be watched and conserved occupying much of the receivers time."[30]

A preliminary notice dated 8 May 1916 was advertised in 'The Nigerian Gazette by Mr Burrowes. The notice also gave a clear picture of the extent of German assets expected to 'fall under the hammer':

The auctioneer is born

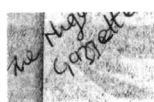

PUBLIC NOTICE.

SALE OF GERMAN GOODS.

G. L. GAISER—LOOSE STOCKS, LAGOS.

Notice is hereby given to the Public that **Mr. A. W. THOMAS, LICENSED AUCTIONEER,** will sell, on behalf of the Receiver, by **PUBLIC AUCTION,** at two o'clock in the afternoon on Thursday, Friday, and Saturday, the 17th, 18th and 19th of December, the **Loose Stocks of G. L. GAISER** in the **COTTON** and **DRY GOODS SHOWROOMS** at **EBUTE ERO** and **IDUMAGBO,** commencing in the cotton showrooms at Ebute Ero.

T. F. BURROWES,
Receiver.

Receiver's Office,
Marina, Lagos,
8th December, 1914.

Public notice on the sale of German assets 'The Nigerian Gazette' – December 1914 G. L. Gaiser - Loose stocks, Lagos

The Colourful Black Auctioneer

The Nigerian Gazette

PUBLIC NOTICE.

SALE OF GERMAN GOODS.

G. L. GAISER and WITT & BUSCH— LOOSE STOCKS, LAGOS.

Notice is hereby given to the Public that Mr. A. W. THOMAS, LICENSED AUCTIONEER, will sell, on behalf of the Receiver, by PUBLIC AUCTION, at Two o'clock in the afternoon on Wednesday, the 13th of January, 1915, the **Loose Stocks of G. L. GAISER and WITT & BUSCH** at Ibadan, commencing in the shop of G. L. Gaiser.

T. F. BURROWES,
Receiver.

Receiver's Office,
Marina, Lagos,
8th December, 1914.

Public notice on the sale of German assets 'The Nigerian Gazette' – December 1914 - G. L. Gaiser & Witt & Busch – Loose Stocks, Lagos

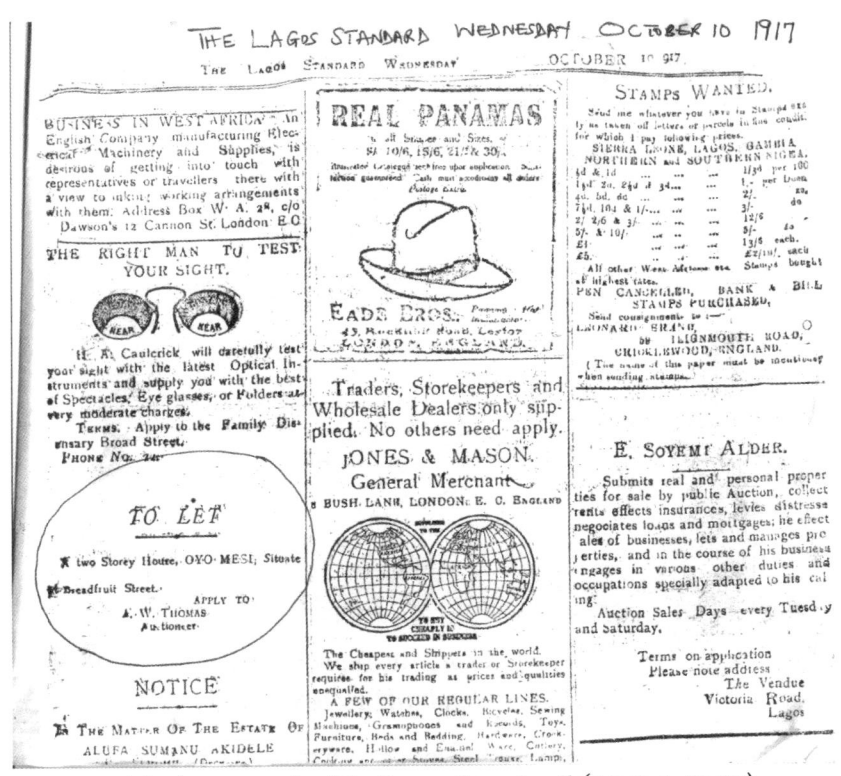

Ad for 'Oyo Mesi' – 'The Lagos Standard' (10 Oct. 1917)

"By order of the Supreme Court, arrangements are being made for the sale of all the Freehold and Leasehold Property of enemy firms in Nigeria, including lands, houses, offices, shops, warehouses, stores, sheds, wharves, piers and all other buildings or fixtures whatsoever, as well as the Trade Marks and Good Will of the various businesses which are now vested in the Receiver…"

Giving indication of the German companies that owned the assets and their nature of businesses, the notice continued:

"The firms carried on a very extensive business, as Shipping agents, Import and Export Merchants, Commission Agents … They were established at all trading centres of any importance in Nigeria, in some cases

Front page ad of A W Thomas & Co
- The Lagos Standard (19 Feb 1896)

for over a quarter of a century and in the case of G.L Gaiser for over sixty years."

The notice also referred to the strategic location of the German businesses:

"The properties are most favourably situated for business purposes, and in some cases it is difficult for the public to obtain other sites ..."

A number of entries on the auction of Germany's assets in Nigeria were made in the Register of Correspondence, a document which was used to catalogue correspondence between the colonial government in Lagos and the Colonial Office in London.

Entry dated 3 August 1916 advised:

"In case the prices range low at the projected auction sale. Considers

The auctioneer is born

that the Nigerian Government should have an agent at the sale with instructions to bid up to ¾ of the valuation on certain properties of value to Government."

Entry made on 27 October 1916, with the heading "Sale of Enemy Properties. Lots with Reserve Prices":

"In minute by Receiver covering statement of Reserve prices. Discusses question of Government purchase of certain lots. Has authorised receiver to bid up to Reserve price for Gainer's No. 23 Marina and Witt and Busch's 2 Tinubu Square…"

Nigeria appeared to be the 'pilot' for the sale of 'enemy' assets. But that policy was deemed fit to be applied globally. In a December 1916 entry in a General Colonial Office document, Sir G Fiddes wrote:

"…As regards our present enemies we shall everywhere have an ordinance, as in Nigeria, to provide that enemy property now sold to

**The Nigerian Shipping Corporation ad
- The Lagos Standard, Jan 1909**

anyone shall never revert to an enemy. If by chance such an Ordinance is incompatible with the terms of peace, it can easily be repealed."

Apart from the auction of Germany's assets during World War One, Andrew Thomas' company valued, auctioned and sold a wide range of goods – from land and buildings to jewellery, furniture, clothing, equipment, etc – and across different civilizations. One of such transactions was the letting of 'Oyo Mesi', a two storey building on Breadfruit Street on the island of Lagos. Being from Oyo himself, I wonder if the building's name had any part in getting him interested in that piece of work.

There was a 'TO LET' advert in the 10 October 1917 issue of 'The Lagos Standard'

There is evidence that Andrew Thomas fully appreciated the power of the media in building his business. A. W Thomas & Co. was one of the regular advertisers in Lagos newspapers from the time the business was set up in 1891 till close to his death in 1924.

Reviewing the positioning of his company's adverts, he started with middle pages which would have attracted relatively lower rates. Media buyers and planners of today would call that 'run of pages (ROP). Notable auctioneers of that era, including J P Haastrup and C Dawodu, were also using middle pages. He later, alongside his competitors, moved to the back page. Just like adverts on the outside back cover (OBC) of magazines of today attracts a higher rate than the ROP, the shift of adverts to the back page of the newspapers would have meant a bigger budget for promotion.

In February 1896, and possibly from a bit earlier, A W Thomas & Co did a marketing twist to out-manoeuvre his competitors. The business went straight for the front page and, at least for some time, was the only auctioneers, valuers and estate agents on the advertisers' dream page. He must have weighed the additional cost of advertising on the front page against the potential benefits. Other companies on the front page of 'The Lagos Standard', issue of 19 February 1896, included The Bank of British West Africa, Aucheterlonie & Sons of West George Street, Glasgow, Scotland and John Walkden & Co of Minshull Street, Manchester, England – wine, spirits and cigar merchants.

In addition, Andrew Thomas appeared to be a business advertiser with a conscience. The 'Record' newspaper was established in 1890, just a year before A W Thomas & Co was set up. It was generally considered the only viable newspaper for business advertising at the time, and it enjoyed the patronage of A W Thomas & Co, among others. In 1895, Andrew W Thomas moved his advertising budget to a new newspaper, 'The Standard', founded in late 1894. A key reason for this change was the fact that the 'Record' was considered to be increasingly pro-government and so less critical of government policies and initiatives. Omu (1978) made this point:

"Among the losses of the Record in 1895, for example, were J. P. Haastrup and A. W. Thomas, both auctioneers."

Andrew Thomas was not only media savvy in terms of advertising, he also built close relationships with key media figures. One of such people was James Bright Davies, a distinguished journalist who established the 'Nigerian Times' in early 1910 (renamed 'Times of Nigeria' in January 1914). Like Andrew W Thomas, he too had worked for the colonial government. When A W Thomas was vice president of the Lagos chapter of the Aborigines Protection Society, J B Davies was the Corresponding Secretary.

There was another significant business enterprise, apart from auctioneering, in which Andrew Thomas had much involvement. He was the Chairman of the Nigerian Shipping Corporation, founded in 1909, with authorised capital of £20,000. The public offer of shares for this business was well advertised. Advert in the 27 January 1909 issue of 'The Lagos

Standard' identified the other key figures in this business.

They included J H Doherty, S Herbert Pearse, W F Lumpkin and Prince Ladapo Ademola. The journalist, James Bright Davies, was Secretary and O. A Sapara Williams, Barrister at Law, as Solicitors.

Oral history shared in the family has it that Andrew Thomas also invested heavily in palm oil export. Sadly, one of his shipments was said to be lost in deep seas and almost caused him financial ruin.

Chapter 5

Petesi Anduru

Let me start by 'decoding' this chapter's heading, for the benefit of readers who do not understand Yoruba, one of the main Nigerian languages.

Petesi – refers to a building with more than one floor. So, if not a bungalow (or a bunker), it would have to be a petesi.

Anduru – the 'Yoruba-nised' version of Andrew

However, the literal meaning conveyed by a simple combination of these two words will not divulge Lagosians' appreciation of the size and beauty of Andrew W Thomas' home. In this context, petesi refers to 'very big, multi-level building'. Basically, you need to inject a bit of oomph to the literal meaning, so as to differentiate it from a basic two-level building.

End of Yoruba lesson. Class dismissed. Sorry, let's make it a short break. Few more Yoruba words to come.

Built in 1913, Andrew W Thomas named his palatial home 'Ebun House' ... oops, break over!... 'Ebun' being a Yoruba word for gift. Doubt if Santa anywhere in the world can wrap a gift that big and concrete, not even with the help of Santa's reindeers. His choice of 'Ebun' had spiritual undertone, a reference to God as owner of heaven and earth. The long version would have been 'Ebun Oluwa' meaning God's gift. Interestingly, Lagosians have a name of their own for the building, and *Petesi Anduru* it was.

Andrew Thomas' home did not escape the attention of historians and researchers. Webster (1964) wrote:

Ebun House (petesi Anduru)
"... a large residence, Ebun House, decorated with fine plaster work by the Brazilian craftman, Balthazar."

Writing more specifically about Lagos and its buildings with 'character', Akinsemoyin and Vaughan–Richards (1977) commented on Ebun House:

> "One of the finest of the late Brazillian houses, covered with the most ornate plasterwork."

Macmillan wrote concerning not just the physical attributes of the house but also its iconic social status:

> "... his palatial home, Ebun House, that towers so loftily above the Lagos houses, the mansion where great native chiefs are entertained when they come to the town, testifies eloquently to the success he has achieved".

To reinforce Macmillan's comment, family oral history has it that when Lagosians hear the kakaki (the special trumpet used by the king's 'town crier'/announcer), they know instantly that king, chiefs and the noble have once again assembled at Andrew's mansion. I can imagine quality food, drinks and entertainment beginning to flow ceaselessly in a golden flood. Business deals, networking, news and jokes rising above the tide. Such was the reputation and status of *Petesi Anduru* while the 'Lord of the Manor' ruled.

The building was like a high rise to Lagosians then, so much so that they had a saying:

'Alamoga bi petesi Anduru'

This draws a comparison between the height of Andrew's building to something, story or an issue considered to be 'high' or exaggerated.

Ebun House had four floors and about 40 rooms. The mansion was made more imposing by a cupola, a dome-like structure, at its very top. The cupola later developed a structural defect and was consequently removed. There was also a pitanga and rose garden.

Lagosians were so intrigued by the towering presence of Andrew

Thomas' home that they placed bets to prove their knowledge of the building. Late Chief Adeniran Ogunsanya, a Lagos State Commissioner for Education in the 1970's once told a story while giving a talk to students of Methodist Boys High School, Lagos in 1973.[31] He said a group of students, including himself, were wondering if a sharp nail could penetrate the walls of Andrew Thomas' mansion. There was divided opinion, and so a bet was placed. The 'trial' saw the nail give up the ghost as the concrete walls proved too strong for its 'claws'. Can't remember if the young Adeniran and his team lost their lunch stipends in the bet.

Situated on Odunfa Street on the island of Lagos, the mansion stretches to the corner of Swamp Street, few metres away from the major Adeniji Adele Road. Adjacent to 'Ebun House' is Thomas Street, named after Andrew Thomas. Oral history has it that the naming of the adjacent road 'Thomas Street' was a compromise, though he owned properties on that street too. The main road on which Andrew Thomas' mansion was situated was to be named after him, but this was not approved due to the religious significance of the street name 'Odunfa'. A shortened form for 'Odun ifa' (meaning the celebration of ifa festival), ifa being the oracle. Popular mainly among the Yoruba, ifa oracle is traditionally used to see where the human eye cannot reach, to unravel a mystery or to predict the future.

Andrew Thomas' decision to build the house in that area of Lagos was a surprise to many people, as the area was very swampy and would cost a lot to fill. But there was no doubt that if he wanted to, he could … and he did. But it was an expensive decision. Some reckoned the money spent in getting the foundation right and filling the land would have been enough to build another big house, perhaps not as big as the mansion that later stood on the fortified swamp. Herbert Macaulay, his close friend and Nigeria's foremost surveyor, was in charge of the survey and helped supervise the building of Ebun House.

The success that graced the career of Andrew Thomas brought him wealth, a lot of it. As we will find out in chapter eight, he gave land and houses in his will. But there was something special about Ebun House. It was his home, and he wanted it to remain in the family – from generation to generation. He therefore gave a directive in his will that his mansion that has become a notable landmark in Lagos must not be sold, but should remain the family home.

Lagosians, and in deed Nigerians as a whole, would have loved the skyline of Lagos to eternally enjoy the radiance of Andrew's mansion. Sadly, it was not to be. After its interiors entertained the noble and kings, and its exterior fascinated the rest of Lagosians for about 70 years, the mansion was sadly reduced to rubble in a fire accident in the early 1980's. Strangely enough, Andrew Thomas himself lived for about seven decades. Just as the inscription on Andrew Thomas' gravestone philosophises that he was 'not lost', the dust of Petesi Anduru shall rise again.

Chapter 6

Better build Bethel big: championing 'Africanism' in the church

Remember the Lagosians banter 'alomoga be petesi Anduru', referred to in the last chapter above? Well, Andrew Thomas' taste for building it big was not limited to 'Ebun House', his residential mansion. When the African Church Bethel was divided as to the size of church they should build, guess where Andrew Thomas casted his lot? Precisely! But before we look more closely into 'better build Bethel big', literally, let us take a few steps back in examining how and why African Church Bethel came into being and the role of Andrew Thomas in all that.

It was like a bolt from the blue, the thunder without the tell tale sign of a lightning. The valedictory service of Bishop James Johnson held at St Paul's Breadfruit, Lagos, a 'flag bearer' of the Church Missionary Society (CMS), on Sunday 13 October 1901 was the setting. A vast number of the Parishioners had hoped Bishop Johnson's tenure as vicar would be extended, but that was not to be.

Bishop Tugwell was said to have made a very undiplomatic move. And that was to challenge Parishioners, that those who were not happy to welcome the new vicar, Rev. Nathaniel Johnson, should leave the church. I doubted if he would have anticipated what happened next. About 600 Parishioners walked out of the church before the valedictory service commenced. As if it was a victory parade or a political rally, they marched out singing. As bees to honey, more people joined this procession of protesters. By the time they arrived at the residence of the Church Warden, Chief Jacob Kehinde Coker, they were numbered about 800.

So, that was how a controllable emotional feeling of 'loss' was catapulted into a protest, resulting into secession from the CMS and the birth of the African Church.

The choice of biblical text for the first ever sermon of the African church[32] is very significant:

"Look not upon me, because I am black, because the sun hath looked upon me; my mother's children were angry with me: they made me the keeper of the Vineyards; but mine own Vineyard have I not kept." (Songs of Solomon 1: 6)

The lay preacher, D J Oguntolu (please don't ask me if he could mix rap and 'juju' music) used the sermon of Sunday 20 October as a rallying cry, admonishing Parishioners that it was now time for Africans to worship God and run churches the African way. It was time for them to 'keep their own Vineyard'.

However, ability to protest and skilful preaching alone would not suffice in establishing a church. The need to add important personalities to the fold was quickly established … deep pockets not required but would be an advantage. Please welcome Andrew W Thomas. Other lobbied VIPs included S A Jibowu, J R Shanu and Fred E Williams.

Andrew Thomas used to be a Parishioner at St Paul's Breadfruit, Lagos, but had moved to Christ Church (another CMS flagship) in nearby Marina before the episode that led to the secession. Initially not too keen on the idea of joining a 'break away' church, he eventually got 'hooked' perhaps on the 'Africanism'. One of the key beliefs that separated the African Church from the European led CMS was the issue of polygamy. Let's add numbers to Andrew Thomas' love of things 'big and beautiful'. With about eight 'wives', a church that would not be overcritical of polygamy would be a breadth of fresh air for him and many others in the same position.

In 1904 Andrew Thomas was appointed Lay President, with D J Oguntolu as his Vice, though the 'Lay' was later dropped in favour of 'President' (I think the latter sounds better!). This appointment may have come as a result of the church constitution, with Andrew Thomas among its chief proponents. The key clergy, now called 'Superintendents', were usually away from Lagos on evangelism, hence the task of administering the church in the clergy's absence fell on Andrew Thomas and his Vice.

We often hear statesmen say religious leaders should stay clear of politics. But for Andrew Thomas, J K Coker and other key lay leaders of the African Church, it was not an issue of church or politics. Sadly, it was politics at its fiercest in church. Aristotle, one of the greatest Greek philosophers, could not have wished for a better demonstration of his *zoon politicus* concept which opined that human beings are by nature political animals. From about 1905, two main camps had emerged in the church. You were either a 'Thomist' or part of Coker's camp.[33] Accusations were matched by counter accusations, and soon, all roads were leading to the courts. Each camp sought the popular vote.

One of the ugliest scenes of the rivalry and division was when the pastor and Chairman of the Church's General Committee, Rev. D C Coates was dismissed by the parish committee and replaced by A.O Ijaoye, a deacon. Coates ignored the dismissal and, with a shield of police officers waiting outside the church, made a 'forced' entry into the church. But the Thomists would not have it. As the newly appointed Ijaoye entered, Coates was carried from the chancel and tossed outside the main door. Political expediency 'metamorphosised' into physical assault. The scene quickly degenerated into a 'free for all' fight, and Coker's camp had to make a hurried exit – through the windows! Not hard to predict that there were yet more law suits.

By 1909, the church had given in to what seemed inevitable. It broke into two – African Church Bethel and African Church Salem. The

Thomists camped at Bethel and the Cokers at Salem. The unifying force of 1901 seemed to have 'gone with the glam' and before the 'cock crow' they had denied the 'brotherhood' that energised them.

Now, let's look at another issue that created division, albeit on a lower scale – the building of Bethel. This was more of congregation versus elders. The majority of 'floor' members of the congregation wanted an imposing storey building while the minority, including the elders and

African Church Bethel, Lagos

the wealthy, wanted a simple, modest church building. But since the elders held the 'purse', their say would have been 'carried'. But there was one little itch. Andrew Thomas decamped. He opted to join the 'floor' majority, and clinched the triumph for them.

The congregation contributed £200. As if he wanted to show he was ready to put his pocket where his mouth was, he quadrupled the congregation's contribution with a payment of £800. But there was a catch – it was a loan. The 'wealthy minority' was led by Dada Adesigbin who questioned the wisdom of a big church building when the purse of the church was comparable to the stomach of a devotee who had done too much fasting. But the support of Andrew Thomas silenced the minority 'naysayers'. In 1917, he held a mortgage on Bethel for £2000. Though part of the building initially collapsed, the imposing edifice desired by the majority of the congregation was realised.

Akinsemoyin and Vaughan–Richards (1977) commented on the church building:

"Bethel Cathedral ... is the heart of the African church and a memorial to the influential elder, A. W Thomas"

In July 1921, Andrew Thomas had to bite the bullet - well, his presidency did. The General Committee of African Church Bethel alleged "high handedness on the matter of African Communion". He, or more likely his camp, was said to have prevented Superintendent J A Lakeru from conducting service at Bethel on Sunday 12 June 1921. He was given the opportunity to defend his position, but declined the offer. By some strange coincidence, the economic crisis of 1921 had badly hit Andrew Thomas' investments. Though J K Coker was also badly affected by the economic depression, Andrew Thomas' 'pyramid' of stalwarts had additionally crumbled. One of his richest and strongest allies, T B Dawodu, had died.

Better build Bethel big: championing 'Africanism' in the church

Interestingly, the church published an open letter in 'Eko Akete' newspaper issue of 23 December 1922. It was addressed to "A.W Thomas Esq, Ex-President, African Bethel Church Organisation". In the letter, the church wrote:

"It is a thousand pities to note that when circumstances culminated in the resignation of your post in which you have been wielding the presidential baton, these twenty years, we were still in the womb of time."

The letter requested Andrew Thomas to:

"… bury the hatchet by overlooking all what had passed which rightly or wrongly has been distasteful to you, and once more, to cast your lot with the organisation with which you have thought it fit to identify yourself".

The church then asked the rhetorical question:

"Would you sign again for the 'flesh pots of Egypt?' Perish the thought!!!"

The letter was rounded up by asking him to:

"Think … and remember your many years' devoted services"

One can only hope that the reconciliatory tone of this letter had struck the 'communion chord' in Andrew Thomas, and helped to put the not-so-pleasant bits of his church presidency behind him. He barely lived a year after the publication of this letter.

Chapter 7

Safeguarding civil rights: membership of Aborigines Protection Society

The Aborigines' Protection Society was founded in 1837. In 1909, it merged with the Anti-Slavery Society and so became known as the Anti-Slavery and Aborigines' Protection Society. Based in Britain, the Society extended to various British colonies and campaigned against various forms of slavery that outlived parliamentary abolition (1807 in Britain and 1833 in British colonies).

The Society also campaigned against the violation of civil rights and unfair laws. One of such laws was the Crown Lands Bill, promulgated in 1894. The purpose was to vest in the British monarch (Queen Victoria was reigning monarch then) ownership and/or control of all unused and unoccupied forest lands and minerals. This measure would of course generate revenue for the Crown through sales and leases of the land. This power would invariably usurp the right of community leaders, traditional rulers and Chiefs as well as landed gentries, particularly in the colonies. The strong opposition that greeted the January 1895 publication of the Bill was therefore predictable. One of the early concerns of the Society in the colonies was therefore to oppose the Bill and any other policies that could potentially erode civil liberties.

The Lagos auxiliary of this pressure group was established, at the invitation of the London-based parent body which was headed by Sir Thomas Fowell Buxton. The primary aim of the group, as contained in Sir Buxton's circular, was "watching over the liberties" of the Crown's subjects. As member of the Lagos branch, and later Vice President,

Andrew Thomas worked alongside other members to ensure the rights and liberties of indigenes were protected. It is very probable that his royal link and his acquisition of land and houses may have also contributed to his interest in this body. So, helping others and protecting his own inter-

S H Pearse
Honourary Secretary, Lagos Aborigines Protection Society

est at the same time.

The Aborigines and Protection Society responded to the bombardment of Oyo. This was reported in 'The Lagos Standard' issue of 29 April 1896:

"... the Committee of the Aborigines Protection Society, true to its

tradition, submitted an Appeal to the Right Hon. Joseph Chamberlain, M.P., Secretary of State for the Colonies on current events in British West Africa ... Reference was made to ...Yorubaland and the recent Oyo trouble".

The Lagos auxiliary intervened on various other matters, including disputes among natives that could potentially damage community relations, and made representations to various officers of the Crown. For example, on 8 September 1905, S. H Pearse, Honorary Secretary, wrote a letter to the Acting Governor through his Private Secretary, J. St Vincent Hand. This was regarding a case brought against Chief Arapate by Ogini and referred to Ilesha Council.[34]

In its editorial comment of December 22 – 29 1917, the Lagos Weekly Record wrote concerning the work of the Aborigines Protection Society:

"There is not the least shadow of doubt that the majority of the active and leading members of the Anti-slavery and Aborigines Protection Society are more or less sound on the Native Question; and we venture to hazard the statement that almost all intelligent Natives of every shade of political opinion are filled with intense gratitude for the good work the Society has done and is still doing in safeguarding the ancestral rights of the natives and protecting their lands from spoliation."

Macmillan (1920) ended his one page biography of Andrew Thomas by mentioning this egalitarian and magnanimous role:

"He is, we may add, Vice-President of the Aborigines Protection Society ... "[35]

Specific research materials on Andrew Thomas' membership and vice presidency of the Lagos auxiliary of the Aborigines Protection Society appears very 'thin' on the ground. Nevertheless, I consider this to be a

Safeguarding civil rights: membership of Aborigines Protection Society

very crucial role, the exclusion of which would render this biography grossly incomplete.

Chapter 8

Not lost, but gone before – will, wealth, death

"We have come to this world with nothing, and with nothing shall we return."

Borrowed from the holy book (Bible), these words are a stark reminder of the reality of our journey's end on earth. Accepting this reality like most people, Andrew Thomas proceeded to documenting how his vast wealth should be shared. Made on 2 July 1923, - unknown to him, precisely five months and five days to his death – his final will left no doubts as to his 'take that' wishes.

Though the precise date of his last breath may have been hidden from him, Andrew Thomas must have known he didn't have much time left. Prior to his death on Monday 7 January 1924, he had been very ill for some time. 'The Nigerian Pioneer' newspaper reported in its issue of 11 January 1924:

"The deceased had been, for a long time suffering from a protracted illness"

Unlike the relative few who shared the view that 'portable' properties would be handy in life after death, Andrew Thomas did not attempt to make the last journey saddled with earthly baggage, not even hand luggage. Nothing to check in. I guess it was a smart move – the 'custom cherubims' at the pearl gates won't miss a contraband or the odd excess gram. That may earn a slam or a silent slap!

Quite unusual for Christian burials of this generation, Andrew Thomas was buried the following day after his death. He died in the early hours of 7 January and the burial service was held at 4pm on 8 January at the African Church Bethel, Lagos. This was followed by internment at Ikoyi cemetery. Like the likes of Ebony of today's Lagos, the Philharmonic Band added colour and festivity to Andrew Thomas' 'last journey'.

'The Nigerian Advocate' of 9 January 1924 described the funeral as "fully masonic", adding that the occasion was graced by "all the elite of the Lagos community." The newspaper also described Andrew Thomas as "the leading Auctioneer in Nigeria."

With only a couple of years short of 70, Andrew Thomas had built himself a phenomenally wealthy estate. So, writing his will must have been quite tasking. But, in the words of William Shakespeare, "the labor we delight in physics pain."[36]

A close look at his will reveals a total of 36 landed properties, the majority of which were houses. This count relates to properties specifically mentioned in the will and so excludes the unspecified number of "residue of my – real and personal property."

In his will, Andrew Thomas divided the properties into three main categories – family, joint and individual. At the top of the list of family properties was 'Ebun House', his 40 room mansion. He was explicit in his wish regarding the family properties:

"It is my earnest wish that my family property shall never be sold, and I hereby request those entitled thereto to strictly observe this my wish."

Included in the long list of property gifts were separate land and building situated at Broad Street in the central business district of Lagos – more like properties in Bond Street, London or Manhattan in New York. On the Broad Street land now stands the 'Western House' office tower. There were seven houses/land on Odunfa Street alone, two in the adjacent Thomas Street (named after him) and four other landed properties in the same vicinity. His property 'empire' extended to the island

The Colourful Black Auctioneer

Gravestone of Andrew Thomas – Lagos

and mainland of Lagos as well as Ibadan, the largest city in West Africa.

Now the 'raw' thing; cash. Over £1300 pounds was shared among beneficiaries. The largest award of £500 went to the African Church Bethel, Lagos. The purpose of the cash gift to the church could not be more specific:

"… to establish a branch of the said Church at Oyo, the capital of Yoruba land."

Despite living most of his adult life in Lagos, Andrew Thomas was proud of his town of origin, Oyo. Even his gravestone reiterates the same point: "A native of Oyo".

The smallest cash award in his will was "seven shillings and six pence (7/6d)", approximately three-quarters of a pound. This amount was very symbolic. This was said to be the precise amount charged by grave diggers at the time!

Now, let us attempt to find out the purchasing power of money in 1923 Nigeria vis-à-vis the value of that amount of money and properties in today's economy. The will itself lends a hand in this quest. Andrew Thomas willed a piece of land in Lagos to a beneficiary and gave something extra:

"…and £50 which my Trustees shall spend in building small house thereon for her."

But how do you define a "small house"? Well, for a man who lived in a 40 room mansion, a four bedroom house may be a very small house. But let's lower the scale. Let us assume the "small house" was a two bed bungalow. To build one today will set you back by about 2 million naira, on the average. That's over $16,000 (US) or £8000 (UK). Worth adding that the value of the Nigerian pound was, for many years in the past, same or higher than the British pound – even as recent as the 1970s. So, how did much gap creep in between the value of the British pound and the Nigerian naira? That's a discussion to be led by experts in economic history, finance and other relevant fields.

So, if £50 in 1923 is now about N2 million by our crude estimation, £1300 at that time would be N52 million. That's $416,000 (US) or £208,000 (UK). So, if our approximation of Andrew Thomas' cash gift in his will is now worth $416,000, what would be the value of the over 36 properties (houses and land, including the 'Ebun House' mansion), he dished out? Now, that would be simply mind blowing, head spinning, eyes dazing, dazzling and …. anybody got paracetamol?

'The Nigerian Advocate' newspaper – issue of 23 January 1924, attempted the daunting task of valuing the whole estate of Andrew Thomas

A section of Andrew Thomas' gravestone
"Not lost, but gone before"

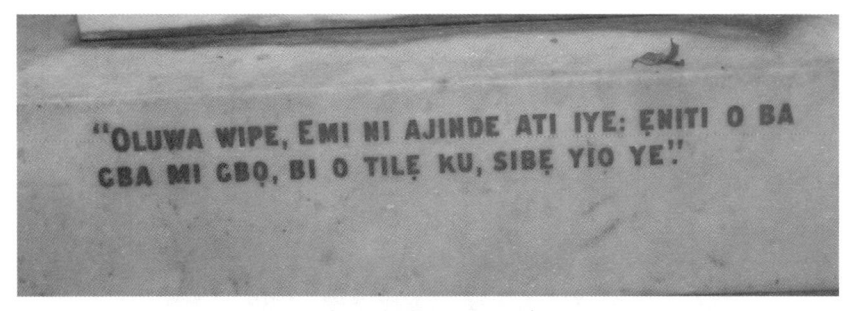

A section of Iwolode Thomas' gravestone
(Biblical inscription in Yoruba)
Oluwa wipe, 'Emi ni ajinde ati iye. Enikeni ti o ba gbamigbo, bio tile ku, yio ye

as presented in his will:

"The Will of the Late Mr Andrew Wilkinson Thomas …the estate which runs up to about hundred thousand pounds, roughly speaking."

This 'dumbed down' estimate, using our rudimentary scale, would be approximately N4 billion in today's economy. That's equivalent to $32 million (US) or £16 million (UK).

There are other aspects of the will that can further enhance our understanding of the personality of Andrew Thomas and the things that mattered to him.

The importance of education and professionalism was clearly evident from the will. He stipulated how proceeds from properties he left for two of his grandchildren who were minors at the time should be used:

"My Trustees shall … apply the same towards their maintenance and professional education till they are qualified as medical doctors, and if they fail, then as lawyers, or in any other useful profession."

Another interesting observation was his specific reference to the poor and needy. Read together with his donation to the church, it paints a

Andrew W Thomas

picture of a man with a charitable nature:

"Any of my personal property not required should not be sold but should be given by my Trustees to the poor in Lagos"

The will also portrayed him as a strict disciplinarian, a no-nonsense man – perhaps to a fault. Commenting on the level of discipline he expected of his family, he wrote:

"….herein after called my family ... to reside therein for life, on condition that if any of my family's conduct … is not conducive to the peace and harmony of my family in my said dwelling house, my Trustees … shall have power to eject such family from my said dwelling house …"

His gravestone exposes one of his strong Christian beliefs – 'life' after death. The inscription, as shown below and used as the main heading of this chapter, may have been chosen by him. So, a philosopher may have once lived among us, yet we knew him not:

Reading the inscription on the gravestone of his father, John Iwolode Thomas, I cannot but notice the vivid similarity of this Christianity influenced philosophical position:

The inscription is a bible passage from John 11:25. The English translation reads:

"I am the resurrection and the life. He who believes in me will live, even though he dies."

The biblical inscription on Iwolode's gravestone seemed to have been crisply summarised by the "Not lost, but gone before" inscription on Andrew's. Both embraced the promise of resurrection, as a key 'pillar' of the Christian faith. What can I say? Like father like son, even unto death.

NOTES

Chapter 1

1. Oni of Ife is the other Yoruba king considered to be of similar status with the Alafin of Oyo.
2. Webster, The African Churches among the Yoruba 1888-1922, p.163.
3. Oral history originally shared by Late Mrs Janet Folorunsho Thomas, daughter-in-law to William Odunaro (one of Andrew Thomas' older brothers). Mrs Janet Thomas lived in Oyo for many years.
4. Law, The Oyo Empire, C.1600 – C. 1836. A West African Imperialism in the Era of the Atlantic Slave Trade. p.121.
5. See Notes no.2 above
6. Interview with a relative (Oyekan Thomas) resident in Oyo. September 2007.
7. Abe means 'under'. Okuta means 'stone/rock.' Abeokuta, in western Nigeria, therefore means the town 'under the rock'. There is a massive rock in Abeokuta known as Olumo rock.
8. Atanda, The New Oyo Empire – Indirect Rule and Change in Western Nigeria. pp.107-109
9. Ibid.
10. Confidential memo, dated 29 January 1915, sent from Government House, Nigeria to the Rt. Hon. Lewis Harcourt, MP, P.C (secretary

of State for the Colonies).

11. www.cms-ogs.org – the website of CMS Grammar School (Lagos) Old Students Association.

CHAPTER 2

12. Bing et al, Makers of Modern Africa – Profiles in History, pp 743-4
13. E-mail correspondence (10/10/07) received from Middle Temple (archive department), London.
14. Senior Advocate of Nigeria (UK equivalent: QC)
15. Narrated by the late Tunde Thomas to my brother, Dr Bode Thomas during the latter's visits to Oyo.
16. Interview with Oyekan Thomas in Oyo. September 2007. Narrated brief biography of his father, Jacob Omosalewa Thomas.
17. Interview with Bisi Agbe in Lagos. August 2007. Narrated brief biography of her Mother, Mrs Comfort Agbe, and provided photograph used.
18. Telephone interview with Col. Victor Gamra. Narrated brief biography of his mother, and provided photograph used.
19. Brief biography of Mrs Coker sourced from my mum, Mrs Olabisi Thomas and my brother, Dr Bode Thomas. Photo provided by mum from the family album.

Chapter 3

20. A brand of chocolate made by Nestle, with the pay off line/slogan: Have a break, have a kit kat.
21. A series of waves created when an ocean 9or other bodies of water) is rapidly displaced.
22. Public relations
23. Reference to James Bond (spy) films

Chapter 4

24. Government Gazette No. 1 of 1891
25. Gass, B & Gass, D, The Word for Today, p.46
26. Macmillan (ed), The Red Book of West Africa, p.104
27. Osuntokun, Nigeria in the First World War, p.24
28. National Archives, Surrey, England. CO 583, 1915.
29. Ibid, CO 583, 1916
30. Telegram sent by Lord Lugard and received at the Office of the Secretary of State for the Colonies on 3 March 1915.

Chapter 5

31. Narrated by my brother, Dr Bode Thomas, who was then an 'A' level student at the school.

Notes

Chapter 6

32. Dada, A History of the African Church, p.13

33. Webster, The African Churches among the Yoruba 1888 – 1922, pp.163-4

Chapter 7

34. File on Aborigines Protection Society, Nigerian National Archives, Ibadan.

35. Ibid

Chapter 8

36. Macbeth – Act 1, Scene 3.

Bibliography

Books

Akinsemoyin, K & Vaughan-Richards, A (1977). *Building Lagos.* 2nd ed., Jersey: Pengrail

Akinwunmi, O (2002). *The Colonial Contest for the Nigerian Region, 1884 – 1900 – A history of the German participation.* Munster: Lit Verlag

Atanda, J A (1973). *The New Oyo Empire – Indirect Rule and Change in Western Nigeria 1894 – 1934.* London: Longman.

Bing, A, Derrick, J & Matatu, G (eds.) (1991). *Makers of Modern Africa – Profiles in History.* 2nd ed. London: Africa Books.

Calvert, A F (1916). *The German African Empire,* London: T W Laurie

Crowder, Michael (1968). *West Africa under Colonial Rule.* London, Hutchinson.

Dada, S A (1986). *A History of the African Church.* Ibadan, Aowa Printers & Publishers

Iyanda, O (ed.) (1989). *The Lagos Chamber of Commerce and Industry under the Nigerian Economy: 1888 – 1988.* Ibadan: Bookcraft.

Kopytoff, J H (1965), *A Preface to Modern Nigeria – The "Sierra Leonians" in Yoruba, 1830 -1890,* Madison and Milwaukee: The University of Wisconsin Press.

Law, R (1977). *The Oyo Empire, C.1600 – C. 1836. A West African Imperialism in the Era of the Atlantic Slave Trade.* Oxford: Clarendon Press.

Le Seur, G (1915), *Germany's Vanishing Colonies,* New York: McBride,

Bibliography

Nast & Co.

Macmillan, A (ed.) (1920). *The Red Book of West Africa*. London: Frank Cass.

Newbury, C W (1961). *The Western Slave Coast and its Rulers – European Trade and Administration among the Yoruba and Adja-speaking peoples of South-western Nigeria, Southern Dahomey and Togo*. Oxford: Oxford University Press.

Ohaegbulam, F U (2002). *West African Responses to European Imperialism in the Nineteenth and Twentieth Centuries*. Lanham: University Press of America.

Omu, F I A (1978). *Press and Politics in Nigeria, 1880 – 1937*. London: Longman.

Osuntokun, Akinjide (1979), *Nigeria in the First World War*, London: Longman.

Webster, J B (1964). *The African Churches among the Yoruba 1888 – 1922*. Oxford: Clarendon Press.

Newspapers

Eko Akete (10/01.1925), In Memoriam

Eleti- Ofe (09/01/1924), p.4

The Lagos Standard (06/02/1895), p.4

The Lagos Standard (12/02/1896), p.1

The Lagos Standard (29/04/1896). 'The Aborigines Protection Society and the Oyo Tragedy'.

The Lagos Standard (27/01/1909), p.3

The Lagos Standard (10/02/1909), p.3

The Nigerian Advocate (09/01/1924), Obituary

The Nigerian Advocate (23/01/1924), Daily Notes, p.5

The Nigeria Chronicle (1908 – 1915), Microfilm. British Library, M.C. 1808

The Nigerian Pioneer (1914 – 1934). Microfilm, British Library, M.C. 1794

The Nigerian Pioneer (29/02/1924), Notice, p.14

The Nigerian Pioneer (11/01/1924), Deaths, p. 3

The Nigerian Times (1914 -1920). Microfilm, British Library, M.C. 1806

The Times of Nigeria (18/04/1921), 'The Present Depression in Trade', p.5

Documents

Anderson, J & Webb, S (1887, 1888). Colonial Office List – Historical and statistical information respecting the colonial dependencies of Great Britain. London: Harrison & Sons

Andrew W Thomas, final will, Lagos - 2 July 1923.

Ashekunowo, S I (compiled 1976). 'List of Photographs in Special Archives Division'. Ibadan: Nigerian National Archives.

Church Mission Society (CMS), Nigerian National Archives, Ibadan. Books 1 & 2

Colonial Office (1915). "Enemy Firms", National Archives, Surrey, England CO583

Colonial Office: Lagos, Original Correspondence (1861 -1906)

Bibliography

– National Archives, Surrey, England. CO147.

Colonial Office: Lagos, Government Gazettes (1881 – 1906) – National Archives, Surrey, England, CO 150.

Colonial Office: Southern Nigeria Protectorate Government Gazettes (1900 – 1913). National Archives, Surrey, England. CO 591/1-12

Colonial Office, General (17 Oct – 31 Dec. 1916), p.62, National Archives, Surrey, England

E-mail correspondence from A Whitelaw (Archivist), Middle Temple, London. Received 10/10/07

Fairfield, E & Anderson, J (1878-79, 1882, 1885). 'Colonial Office List – Historical and statistical information respecting the colonial dependencies of Great Britain'. London: Harrison & Sons (Printers in Ordinance to her Majesty)

Gass, B, Gass, D & Halliday, R G (May – July 2007), 'Changing Lives for Good – The Word for Today'. Lagos: Grace So Amazing Foundation.

Memo (confidential), dated 29 January 1915, sent from Government House, Nigeria to the Rt. Hon. Lewis Harcourt, MP, P.C (secretary of State for the Colonies). National Archives, Surrey, England. CO 7903

Microfilm (21/07/1916) 'Enemy Property in Nigeria', CAB 37/152

Nigeria Register (1916) – Register of correspondence from the colonial government in Nigeria to the Foreign Office, London. National Archives Surrey, England (Ref: 578, 36630)

Payne, J A O (1893). 'Table of Principal Events in Yoruba History, with certain other matters of general interest', Lagos.

Photographs. Nigerian National Archives, Ibadan. OSP 1/CMS

Simple List of Lagos Colony Records. Ibadan: Nigerian National Archives.

Simple List of Oyo, Provincial Papers. Ibadan: Nigerian National Archives

Telegram – from the Governor-General of Nigeria (Lord Lugard) to the Secretary of State for the Colonies (Rt. Hon. Lewis Harcourt, PC, MP). Received 3 March 1915. National Archives, Surrey, England. CO 583/31, p.99

The Nigeria Gazette – (supplement to Gazette No. 25, 1 June 1916), "German and Austrian Firms", p.mlii

Websites

www.allafrica.com/stories/200709250974.html - accessed 03/08/07

www.antislavery.org – accessed 02/08/07

www.cms-ogs.org – accessed 26/07/07

www.proquest.co.uk – accessed 03/07/07

Oral history and interviews

Different sources/interviewees, mostly within the Andrew Thomas extended family.